THE SECRET ART OF BEING A GROWN-UP

TIPS, TRICKS, and PERKS NO ONE THOUGHT to TELL YOU

THE
SECRET
ART OF
BEING A
GROWN-
UP

TIPS, TRICKS, and PERKS NO ONE THOUGHT to TELL YOU

BRIDGET WATSON PAYNE

CHRONICLE BOOKS
SAN FRANCISCO

Library of Congress Cataloging-in-Publication Data available.

ISBN 978-1-4521-5313-1

Manufactured in Canada

Designed by Rachel Harrell
Illustrations by Rachel Harrell

10 9 8 7 6 5 4 3

Chronicle Books LLC
680 Second Street
San Francisco, California 94107
www.chroniclebooks.com

FOR MABEL, WHO'S GOING TO NEED
THIS BOOK IN ABOUT TWENTY YEARS.

Hello, grown-up!

WELCOME TO THIS BOOK!

It doesn't matter if you've officially been an adult for five minutes or five years or twenty-five years. It's never too soon, and never too late, to claim the rights and privileges of being a grown-up. Whereas the world decides that you are an adult at 18 or 21 or whatever, grown-up-hood is not something conferred by outside powers, it is something you lay hold of for yourself. Because here's the secret:

Whereas being an adult is a lot of hard work, being a grown-up is fun.

We all intuited this when we were little kids, didn't we? We imagined that when we were grown-ups we would not be boring like our parents. No, once we were allowed to do whatever we wanted, we would take full advantage of that prerogative. We would eat all the candy. We would stay up late watching TV. We would let the dog sleep in the bed with us. And let our friends come over and stay for supper, not just once in a while but every gosh darn night!

And the thing is, we were right! Being a grown-up *is* the best. You really do get to eat what you want and do what you want and see your friends when you want. The only catch is that along with being a grown-up comes being an adult, and being an adult is not quite *as* fun. Because being an adult is basically about responsibility—going to work, paying the bills, etc.

So how do we reconcile the fun of grown-up-hood with the responsibilities of adulthood? Well, it turns out it's not really such a dichotomy as at first it seems to be. There are lots of practical tips and tricks and best-practices and work-arounds that grown-ups know that make their adult responsibilities easier and more enjoyable, and that in turn free up more of their time and energy for fun grown-up things like coffee-and-donuts and sleepovers and new haircuts.

However, for some mysterious reason, the tricks for leveling-up your grown-up game are rarely articulated, rarely explained. Parents tend to forget to tell their kids about the tabs on the ends of the tinfoil box (p 23). There are no classes in high school about the dangers of credit card interest (p 38). No college seminars about how to get a group of people to decide where to go for dinner (p 97).

Which is where this book comes in. Domestic life, social life, taking care of yourself, taking care of your finances, navigating the great wide world—being a grown-up means engaging with these matters in ways that are both useful and enjoyable. Reaping the benefits of your age and wisdom. And having at least as good a time while doing so as you thought you would when you were seven.

The Single Greatest Truth that Grown-Ups Know and Teenagers Don't Know:

95% of the time no one is looking at you!

BECAUSE OF THIS:

You can wear whatever the heck you want (see page 18)

You can walk into nice hotels to use the restroom (see page 21)

You can go where you want (see page 46)

And much much more! Read on…

You don't need a garlic press.

BUT AN OMELET PAN MIGHT NOT BE A BAD IDEA...

To actually start cooking really good food that you and your friends will want to eat, you truly need very little equipment. Any kitchen tool that performs only one specific function is highly suspect—these false friends are easy to spot because they usually have the name of the one and only type of food they work on as part of their names. You don't want something that can only work on garlic or donuts or apples. You want something that can do a ton of different jobs in your kitchen.

One exception to this might be a small nonstick pan which is mostly for cooking eggs. But, come on, they're eggs! They're so versatile. You can make about forty different egg dishes in your little pan.

THINGS THE KITCHEN STORE WANTS YOU TO OWN

- Garlic press
- Shrimp de-veiner
- Espresso maker
- Donut pan
- Toaster oven
- Steak knives
- Pancake flipper
- Apple slicer
- Cherry pitter
- Wonton mold
- Mellon baller
- Panini press
- Citrus zester
- Fish spatula

THE 10 THINGS YOU ACTUALLY NEED

- Small nonstick pan
- Larger not-nonstick pan
- Big pot (but not too big—5 or 6 quarts should be fine)
- Wooden spoon
- Good chef's knife
- Colander
- Cutting board
- Spatula
- Measuring cups
- Measuring spoons

90% amazing is still amazing.*

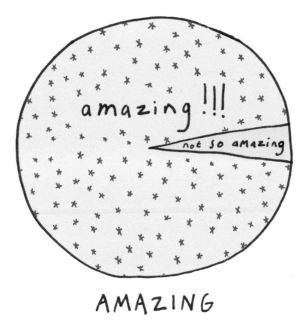

AMAZING

*And the sooner you figure that out the happier you will be.

Put another way:

MAKE FRIENDS WITH IMPERFECTION BECAUSE IT'S ALREADY MADE FRIENDS WITH YOU.

Or, put yet another way:

PERFECTIONISM IS POISON.

Or, put maybe the best way of all:

GOOD ENOUGH IS GOOD ENOUGH.

Take the second, less crowded, bus or train.

We've all seen it happen: Lots of people are waiting at a bus stop or train platform for a vehicle to arrive. Maybe they've been waiting a long time. Eventually it does arrive, and it is crowded. But there is another one right behind it, only waiting for the first one to leave.

And what do people do? They panic, particularly if they've been waiting a while. They tend to freak out and all crowd on to the first one. Off it goes, with the people's faces practically smushed up against the windows.

The second one pulls up, opens its doors, and the few smart people who waited get on sit down and ride to their destination in comfort. And yes, they even get there, at worst, just a few moments later, and often even faster than the folks on the first one.

Be one of the smart people. Don't panic. Be a grown-up. Your commute will thank you.

You can wear whatever the heck you want.

THERE IS NO SUCH THING AS NOT BEING ABLE TO "GET AWAY WITH" OR "PULL OFF" SOMETHING, STYLE-WISE.

You can pull off exactly however much you decide you can pull off. The only person who really cares is you.

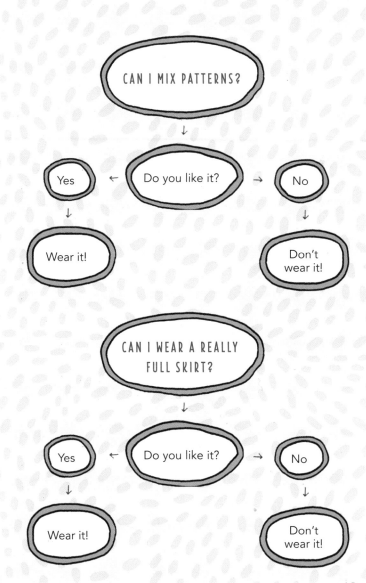

CAN I MIX PATTERNS?

Do you like it? → No → Don't wear it!

Yes ← Do you like it?

Wear it!

CAN I WEAR A REALLY FULL SKIRT?

Do you like it? → No → Don't wear it!

Yes ← Do you like it?

Wear it!

CONCIERGE

You can go into nice hotels to use the restroom.

For real. Just walk right in like you own the place and odds are no one will say a thing about it.

Pro tip: Don't ask where the restroom is. Just walk forward toward the side or back of the lobby, where it logically should be. If you project even a medium level of self-assurance, most likely no one will pay any attention to you at all.

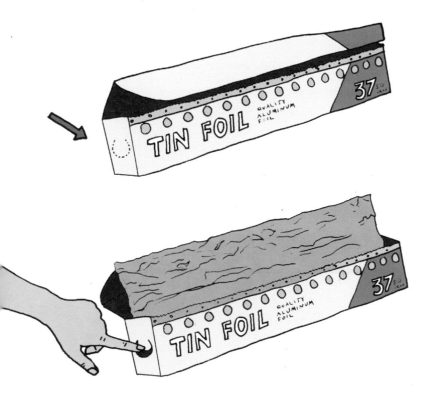

Guess what?

Boxes of aluminum foil, cling wrap, wax paper, and so forth have these little cardboard tabs on the ends of the box that you can push in to keep the roll from falling out.

Taking two seconds to punch them in before you first open the box will save you dozens and dozens of tiny roll-flying-out-of-box frustrations over the lifetime of that particular box in your kitchen.

If you already knew about this before reading this page, well damn, you are way, way ahead of the game.

Pat yourself on the back, grown-up!

*Hint: NOT a chair
you'd see at a party*

Work can, and will, be a drag.

That's why they call it "work" and not "crazy fun time."

And that's why they have to *pay you to be there.*

By all means look for a job you love, but realize there will always be unlovable things about any job.

LEARN TO SAY "WORK SHMERK!"

PEOPLE CAN BE AWFUL.

THEY CAN ALSO BE AWESOME.

Best not to judge.

And *never assume.*

*people who
can be awful* /

people who
can be awesome

/

people

27

You 100% deserve to be loved.

No ifs, ands, or buts.

Repeat this until you believe it.

Everyone gets down sometimes. Maybe a particular set of circumstances—whether trivial or major—is bumming you out. Maybe you're just blue for no reason. Hey, it happens. And sometimes what you need to do is just sit around and mope. And that's fine.

But other times you may want to make yourself feel better. But you may not know how. At this point you might want to attempt one of the most tried and true, time-tested solutions:

Get the heck out your front door.

Get out into the world—that could mean the natural world, like going for a hike in the hills, or it could mean the human-made world, like sitting at an outdoor table with a cup of coffee as people pass by—either way the trick is to look. And not just look, but really *see*.

SEEING THE WORLD AROUND YOU CAN BE THE CURE FOR WHAT AILS YOU.

FOR INSTANCE:

- Look at nature. See the trees and the sky and the clouds and the blades of grass.

- People watch. Consider the lives of others.

- Go for a walk and look carefully at the buildings.

- Go someplace you can look at moving or flowing water and watch how it goes.

- Go to an art museum and look at art.

And just like that, almost like magic, you'll find your consciousness has reoriented itself. Instead of looking inward at your inner problems (which, let's be clear, are totally valid and real), you're looking outward at the world around you. You have pulled off the famous trick of "getting out of your head." Well done.

If ever there's a time for patience, it's when you're cooking.

The temptation to poke and prod at things can be almost irresistible. Emphasis on the *almost*. If you exert your very best most grown-up self-control you'll find you can indeed resist the urge.

And this will be a very good thing because you know what happens to meat you impatiently scrape off the pan (too soon) when it's sticking because *it's not done yet*? All the goodness and flavor gets left behind, stuck to the pan, where it chars away to nothing.

Whereas if you just wait a bit, the meat will easily lift right up when it's ready to do so, bringing all its deliciousness with it.

No doubt there's a larger life lesson embedded in this whole cooking thing as well, all metaphor-like, if you care to look for it. But for now just remember . . .

The meat stops sticking when it's done.

Find someone who explains things to you in a way you understand.

Get this person to explain to you how to do various potentially tricky things, like maybe:

- Play pool
- Make small talk
- Drive a stick shift
- Fold fitted sheets
- Talk about wine
- Gamble
- Give to charity

- Sew on a button
- Volunteer
- Clean the bathtub
- Treat a hangover
- Give a toast
- Stake out space in a crowded room

Odds are your explanations will make sense to them too. So you, in turn, can explain to this person all the tricky things they don't know how to do that you do. It will be a mutually beneficial relationship.

YOU MIGHT ALSO WANT TO GO AHEAD AND MARRY THIS PERSON, WHILE YOU'RE AT IT.

Just saying.

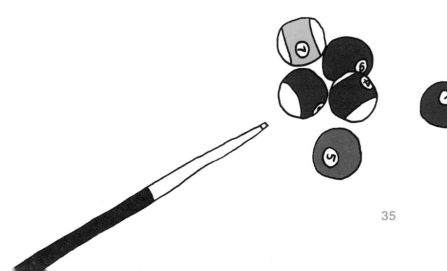

You, yes you, can make stuff and be handy.

ALL YOU NEED ARE TWO IMPORTANT RULES:

Rule #1: Sand and prime

Rule #2: Measure twice

(No, actually, you know what? Go ahead and measure 3 times.)

BONUS ITEM:

1 can of spray paint primer + 1 can of colored spray paint will just cover a small end table, bedside table, shelf, or the like. And it will look good. Like actually really quite good.

Pay your bills on time.

Boring? Yep. Grown-Up? You betcha.

Figuring out a system that works for you to make this happen frees up huge swathes of time and space in your life and brain for things that are way more fun.

But how, you ask? Well, that depends on your problem. Things are about to get a little tough-love around here, but it will for sure be worth it. Grab a coffee, turn the page, and find the piece of pie that's right for you.

WHY BILLS GO UNPAID:

57% *Bills misplaced somewhere in apartment*

1% *Legitimate unavoidable impediment (stuck out of town longer than anticipated when flight is canceled due to volcanic eruption, postal service loses mail in blizzard, etc.)*

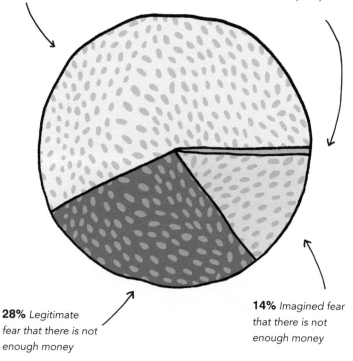

28% *Legitimate fear that there is not enough money*

14% *Imagined fear that there is not enough money*

AND HOW TO FIX THAT:

57% Solution: the landing pad. Have a place right inside your front door to put the mail (and hey, while we're at it, your keys too). Sort through it once a week and pay anything that's coming up due in the next seven days.

14% Solution: Get over your scarcity issues and acknowledge that you are a grown-up. Insolvency is not one water bill way.

28% Solution: For credit card bills—do not pay only the minimum payment! Take the grand total and divide it by 3 months, 6 months, or 12 months (whichever gets you the highest amount you can actually manage to pay) and pay that amount, every month, till the bill is gone. And for god's sake, don't charge anything else in the meantime. Seriously! For other bills—call up the relevant entity and make arrangements before the bill is late. That's what grown-ups do, and the faceless bureaucrats will almost for sure be more helpful at this point than later on.

1% Solution: Pay bill late, move on with your life.

liquid

solid

gas

gas

(same amount)
(smaller container)

Your expenditures are not a solid or a liquid, they are a gas.

THEY CAN EXPAND OR CONTRACT TO FIT THE SIZE OF CONTAINER THEY FIND THEMSELVES IN.

You control the size of the container.

This same principle is also true of the amount of time it takes to get ready in the morning.

Hang up some art.

Many people feel that they are too broke, or too young, or too uncertain about their own taste, or too temporary in their living situation to take the leap of actually hanging up pictures on their walls.

But grown-ups get to have things up on their walls that they enjoy looking at, that make them just that teeny bit happier each and every day. That's part of the deal. You *have* to take out your own recycling, but you *get* to hang up art.

SOMETIMES IT'S NICE TO KNOW THE RULES. HERE THEY ARE:

- Everything goes in a frame. No teenage pushpins.

- Everything is original, no reproductions: photos of people you know, pictures made by people you know, art prints.

- Hang pictures with their centers five and a half feet above the floor ("eye-level" for adult humans).

- To hell with your security deposit. Bang nails into the walls with impunity!

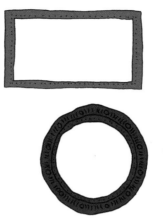

But though these rules have merit and should be deployed whenever they are useful to you, you know what else? Screw the rules. You're a grown-up and you get to do what you want.

HERE ARE THE ANTI-RULES:

- There are amazing grown-up homes full of things-not-in-frames and yes, even pushpins.

- If you find a poster or a postcard or anything else you just adore, slap it in a frame (or not) and put it up!

- Art can look amazing hung way too high or even sitting on the floor and just leaning against the wall.

- Actually there is no reason ever to blow off that last rule. Don't worry about the walls.

Go where you want.

Sometimes you may get the sense from the world that certain kinds of places aren't for you. And while very occasionally this may be true (like, say, the Oval Office), the vast majority of the time this is just so much nonsense. We all have a little kid inside our brains who worries that we might not be *allowed* to

art gallery

fancy restaurant
(white tablecloth, several
forks per person)

go in there, but we are grown-ups now and we can go wherever we want to go. Gently, kindly, tell that little kid to settle down and give these places a try. Some may seem easy to you but others will feel like kryptonite—be brave and try out both.

THESE PLACES (AND MANY, MANY MORE) ARE FOR YOU:

classy bar

farmers market

golf course
(or some other
fancy sports place)

THINGS TO

buy more of before you run out

OF THE ONES YOU'VE GOT:

- paper towels
- ibuprofen
- razor blades
- coffee filters
- toothpaste

- deodorant
- tampons
- condoms
- toilet paper
- butter

THINGS TO
stop feeling embarrassed
ABOUT BUYING:

- jelly donuts
- decaf coffee
- swimsuits
- medicines for conditions sixth-grade boys find funny

*Put the liquid measuring cup into the colander in the sink as a reminder to yourself to use it to scoop out some water from the pot before you drain the noodles—otherwise *everyone* forgets this.

Read the recipe all the way through for booby traps.

In cooking, like in math, it's good to get a handle on the concept of order of operations. Many recipes are full of things they don't tell you till the middle or even the end, but that really need to be done first. If you read the whole thing first, you'll spot stuff like:

- Boiling the pasta water

- Toasting the bread for the sandwiches

- Chopping all the ingre-dients before you start cooking (otherwise known as mise en place)

- Reserving some pasta water*

- Toasting the nuts

- Lining the unbaked pie shell with foil

With shoes, disregard myths about what's cool and go for quality.

FOR GIRLS: Gorgeous, well-made, comfortable flat shoes that you can walk for miles in will make you feel like a fabulous grown-up. Cheap-o heels that give you blisters after five minutes will make you feel like a kid playing dress-up in her mom's closet.

FOR GUYS: Nice leather shoes don't have to read as boring or square or establishment. It's all about how you style them. Worn with jeans, they can make you feel like a fabulous grown-up. Ratty tennis shoes can make you feel five years old.

Dinner parties don't have to be a certain way; they should just be fun. Throw them.

You don't have to know what you're doing. You don't have to be fancy or posh. Just cook some food and invite some friends over to eat it. Then later, do it again. And again. And again. Every time it will get funner and funner and less intimidating. You will be embracing and sharing your grown-up life.

Dinner parties are exactly the sort of thing that can seem out of your reach because you've seen them look a certain way on TV or in a lifestyle magazine, but in fact they are exactly for you because you are a grown-up.

GOOD THINGS FOR DINNER PARTIES:

- Fish (easier than you think)

- Chocolate cake (harder than you think, but worth it)

- Huge pot of spaghetti, garlic bread, salad

- Omelets full of fun things like crab and spinach

- Grilled cheese sandwiches and tomato soup

- Pie (really easy if you buy the crust pre-made)

- Champagne cocktails

- Thai food (homemade or takeout)

- Taco bar

- Penne, tomato, cream, vodka, shrimp

- Breakfast for dinner

- Ice cream sundaes

- Chicken pot pie

- Big Caesar salads (with or without anchovies and chicken)

When opening champagne, prosecco, or the more affordable sparkling wine of your choice (which, by the way, you keep in the fridge at all times, because you never know when cause for celebration may arise) . . .

Turn the bottle, not the cork.

Be generous with the oil,
miserly with the vinegar,
wise with the salt,
and a madman with
the pepper

—PROVERB

Make your own salad dressing.

YOU'LL SAVE MONEY, MAKE SOMETHING TASTY, AND AVOID THE CARDINAL SALAD SIN OF OVERDRESSING.

Yields enough to perfectly dress a generous salad for two.

- **1 tablespoon of the best olive oil you can afford**
- **1 teaspoon vinegar (any kind except white distilled)**
- **pinch of salt (literally, just pinch it up, that's the right amount)**
- **pinch of herbs de Provence (or a single dried herb, such as thyme)**
- **a whole heck of a lot of fresh ground black pepper**

STEP 1:

Stir together the vinegar and salt in a cup.

STEP 2:

Hold a fork or small whisk in one hand and the spoonful of olive oil in your other hand. Simultaneously pour the olive oil slowly, slowly in a narrow stream into the cup while frantically whisking as fast as you can. (This takes a tiny bit of practice to nail down, but do it just a couple of times and you'll totally have it.)

STEP 3:

Stir in the dried herbs and a truly insane-seeming amount of pepper. Taste. If it's too oily add a few more drops of vinegar; if it's too salty or sour add a small pinch of sugar.

Own something nice to wear.

IT FEELS NICE TO LOOK NICE.

And there's going to be that one occasion, at least once a year, when you *really need to look nice.*

Suits and fancy dresses will serve you well for years to come.

(Plus, bonus: they tend to go out of style more slowly than other kinds of garments.)

If you haven't already, do yourself a favor, bite the bullet, and get one now. You deserve it. If money is an issue, it can totally be secondhand.

And if this is not your issue, if in fact you have a closet full of this sort of stuff that you rarely or never wear: it's ok. You can stop shopping now. You're already ready for any eventuality. Good job.

In terms of your living space, think like a curator.

It's okay to accumulate stuff. Books, pictures, mementos. Recipes, spices, wooden spoons. Handbags, neckties, nice socks with no holes in them. As long as what you have is meaningful, beautiful, or useful, keeping it around is perfectly fine.

If you're happy with your space, there is absolutely no need to feel guilty that you have not pared down to three exquisite Japanese T-shirts folded into perfect rectangles.

But here's the secret to maximalism (or even just "mediumism"):

Keep only what matters, and keep it neat and organized.

Weed and curate your possessions regularly. Not to purge down to near nothing, but just to chuck out all the junk that inevitably makes its way into our homes without our permission.

Have a place for everything and put everything into its place as soon as it comes in the door. You should never have to waste even a second of your grown-up life wondering where to put the toilet paper. Or tripping over the toilet paper package where you left it in the hallway.

Avoid gimmicks.

AND

Trust your gut.

Someday someone will invite you to do something that they swear to god is super cool but that you know in your heart of hearts is going to be super lame.

Don't do it.

Does this mean you should never try new things?

Of course not.

Does it mean you should never let yourself be persuaded by a friend to broaden your horizons?

No!

What it does mean is that when someone invites you to a soirée with a theme, and that theme is nothing more or less than the wearing of hats, and every fiber of your being screams that it is going to be a stupid party, your fibers are right. Trust your fibers.

This can all be summed up very, very simply:

NEVER GO
TO A HAT
PARTY.

When it comes to relationships:

DON'T PRETEND EVERYTHING IS GREAT, AND DON'T
PRETEND EVERYTHING IS AWFUL.

Fighting is healthy. But always fight clean.

Top 10 aphorisms for fighting:

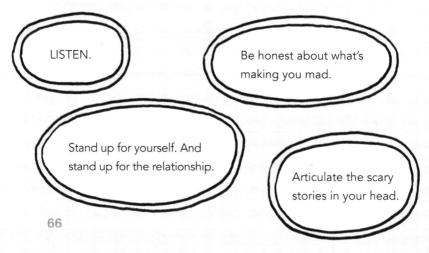

LISTEN.

Be honest about what's making you mad.

Stand up for yourself. And stand up for the relationship.

Articulate the scary stories in your head.

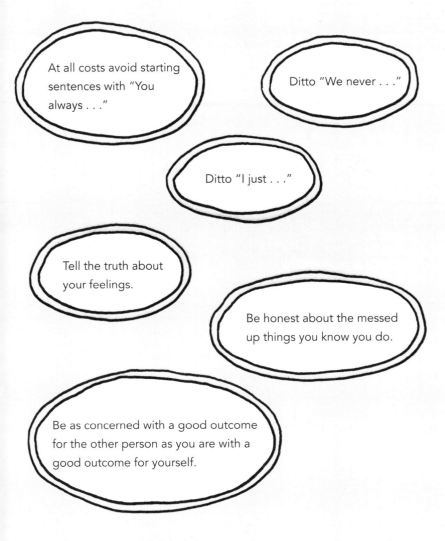

At all costs avoid starting sentences with "You always . . ."

Ditto "We never . . ."

Ditto "I just . . ."

Tell the truth about your feelings.

Be honest about the messed up things you know you do.

Be as concerned with a good outcome for the other person as you are with a good outcome for yourself.

Nearly everything is a continuum, not simply black and white.

don't complain --------- complain

fulfill obligations -------- flake out

be friendly --------- be surly

overindulge --------- don't

This can be a very hard lesson to learn, remember, and truly internalize. Every day you're going to fall at a different place on a number of different continuums. Accept this, and stop beating yourself up. Most days you'll fall somewhere in the middle of these ranges; now and then you'll be way off down at one end or the other—extremely virtuous or extremely not. It's all fine.

This brings us to a maybe even more important precept:

Everything in moderation including moderation.

"Be yourself." People say this all the time, but what does it even mean?

WELL, LOTS OF THINGS, REALLY.

It means:

- Don't do things just because you think you should if deep down you know they're not right for you.

- Don't be a weird person trying to be normal, or a normal person trying to be weird.

- Find a way to defeat the fear that people will like you better if they don't know what you're really, really like.

It can even mean a lot of quite serious, somewhat grim, but deeply important physiological work.

But it can also mean having fun as only you know how to have fun.

Do the things that please the heck out of you.

- Eat cookies for dinner.

- Have a drink.

- Stay up late.

- Sleep late.

- Wake up early.

- Stay home and read a book.

- Go out on lots of dates with lots of different people.

- Call in sick and go sit by the ocean.

- Take up running.

- Take up pottery.

- Take up something you're really, really bad at.

- Make time to do that thing you're really good at.

- Warm up the bath water six times and turn into a prune.

- Get married.

- Don't get married.

You are not your job.

WORK WHEN YOU NEED TO WORK, AND TAKE BREAKS WHEN YOU NEED TO TAKE BREAKS.

You're a grown-up, so you get to determine the balance between what you have to do and what you need.

Is this just an excuse to slack off? No. Trust your judgement. Odds are you have enough money and flexibility to go get a coffee with a friend in the afternoon, especially if you or the friend are having a bad day.

Don't fall into the common work fallacy of convincing yourself that you're indispensable. You are not indispensable.* And you don't want to be indispensable (because someday you want to be able to go do something else amazing).

*At your job, that is. In real life, yes, you are a precious singular snowflake and there has never been and will never be anyone else just like you, ever, and you are indeed utterly indispensable. Just not at work.

As a wise man once said:

Trust the sandwich maker.

THIS IS BOTH A LITERAL TRUTH AND A METAPHORICAL TRUTH.

LITERAL:

If a person has been making sandwiches in the same sandwich place for a number of years, they know the best sandwich to make for you. They know what combination of ingredients is going to taste most delicious. Don't try and come up with some crazy combo of your own—order the special scrawled on the chalkboard or ask them what's good today.

METAPHORIC:

Don't micromanage. Have a little faith in the competence of others. Let people get on with the jobs they are expert at and get the heck out of their way. Trust that you are not the only person in the universe who knows how to do stuff right. Being a grown-up doesn't mean being awesome at everything—it means letting the people who are awesome at something get on with it.

Here's the thing about beauty and grooming:

1. FIGURE OUT THE THINGS THAT ARE REALLY, TRULY REFLECTIVE OF WHO YOU ARE ON THE INSIDE.

2. MAKE THOSE THINGS REAL IN THE PHYSICAL WORLD OF YOUR OUTSIDE.

FOR EXAMPLE:

- If your innermost self has pink hair, have pink hair.

- If your innermost self has a great big lumberjack beard, have a great big lumberjack beard.

- Same goes for makeup, cologne, and of course, apparel.

Not too surprisingly, it turns out to be much easier to actually do these sorts of things at moments in time when they happen to be fashionable or trendy, and that is perfectly okay.

Just also be okay with continuing to have the thing, after it is no longer cool, if it truly does reflect your true self.

Learn the value of long-term-thinking.

Do contribute to a 401k if given the chance.

Do occasionally invest in well-made timeless garments that will last a lifetime.

Do bring to an end states of being (relationships, jobs, living situations, whatever) that not only aren't working for you right now, but, let's be honest, never are going to work.

Don't procrastinate (except when you really, *really* feel like it).

Don't tear apart vintage jewelry thinking you're going to "make something even cooler out of it." You won't. Not ever. The only thing you will achieve is a pile of broken jewelry.

Don't, whatever you do, *do not* stick tape to filing cabinets. It will never come off, never ever ever, no matter what you do, and it will always look like total crap.

Set boundaries.

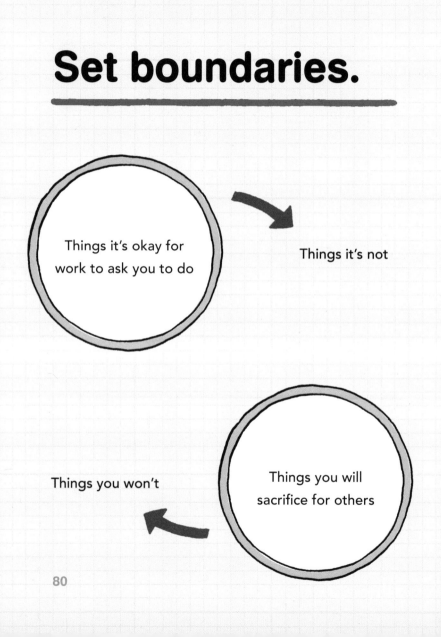

Things it's okay for
work to ask you to do

Things it's not

Things you won't

Things you will
sacrifice for others

Things you don't

Outrageous behavior you put up with from your family members

Bad habits you'll tolerate in a partner

Things you shouldn't

Never underestimate the power of nature.

TIMES TO TAKE THE NATURAL WORLD VERY, VERY SERIOUSLY:

When a trail or ski run is marked EXTREMELY DIFFI-CULT, or the sign at the beach says NO SWIMMING.

When you choose to cohabitate with another organism (be it plant, animal, or human) with its own biological needs and functions.

When doing laundry. 100% cotton, line-dried in the sun, absorbs the amazing smell of sunshine. Seriously. No, really. There is no good way to convey this, you just have to try it.

When everyone is posting pictures of the same amazing sunset outside and you're inside. Stop looking at your phone and go outside!

You can find a way to afford the plane tickets.

Travel is the best. Just the best. Nothing else simultaneously expands your outlook and enriches your inner being so deeply. It's the ultimate win-win.

But loads of people miss out on loads of trips because they convince themselves they can't afford them when, really, they could.

SURE, MAYBE YOU CAN'T AFFORD IT RIGHT THIS VERY SECOND, BUT YOU CAN STILL MAKE IT HAPPEN. HERE'S HOW:

- Save up. Squirrel away a little cash each month, and before you know it, you'll have the cost of a flight.

- Find additional sources of cash: dog-sit, freelance, take a short-term gig on the side, pack your lunch.

- For the love of god, do not charge the plane tickets on your credit card unless you have a very concrete plan about how you're going to pay it off.

We all toss money away on small things but balk at the bigger things. When really, shouldn't it be the other way around?

Which is going to improve your life more? That latte, and the one tomorrow, and the one the day after that? Or Mexico City?

Be thrifty sometimes.

No one really talks about being "thrifty" anymore. People from the 1930s were obsessed with it, and people from the 1970s were pretty darn into it too. But in the twenty-first century it's kinda gone out of fashion.

Which is too bad, because it's a pretty cool concept when you think about it—if you save money on some stuff, that means you will have more money to spend on other better, more important and fun stuff—like, for example, plane tickets!

HERE ARE SOME IDEAS ABOUT HOW TO PULL THAT OFF:

- Make coffee at home and invest in a travel mug (as opposed to buying $4 lattes— $5 after you tip— every day).

- Institute a 48-hour waiting period before downloading any new digital content you get excited about. If you still want it two days later, great, but this will help weed out mistaken impulses.

- Same goes for online shopping for clothes, electronics, stuff for your house, cosmetics, etc., etc., etc.

- Take public transit. Save cabs, ride apps, car sharing, even driving your own vehicle, for times you really need them.

- Avoid paying interest (aka paying the minimum on your credit card bill), for which you get NOTHING in return.

Now and then the solution really is to throw money at the problem.

Not all that often. But now and then.*

And the sneaky thing about this one is that the instances of it increase—again, not a ton, but a bit— as you get older.

Because you can reasonably expect not only your income but also your intolerance for inconvenience to increase as the years go by.

Caveat: We're talking here about money you actually have in your possession. *Avoid credit cards.*

Here's a good rule of thumb:

AFTER 25: HIRE MOVERS

AFTER 30: TAKE CABS TO THE AIRPORT

A SURPRISING FACT ABOUT COOKING AT HOME IS HOW PRICEY CERTAIN ITEMS ARE.

Sure, some things—like wine, where a whole bottle will set you back what a single glass might in a restaurant—are great deals.

But other things—such as meat—can be shockingly expensive.

BUT THERE ARE WORKAROUNDS:

Flank steak is pretty cheap.

So are the smaller, frozen shrimp.

But you know what's even cheaper and in many ways just as impressive? Those big old Portobello mushrooms.

Go veggie for the night (or forever) and save yourself a world of trouble.

Just a thought.

HAVE YOU WORKED IN FOOD SERVICE?

If the answer is yes, you don't even need to bother with reading the opposite page. You already know what to do.

If the answer is no, go do that.

Then come back and read this page again.

Overtip.

Don't be tempted by that Sunday night red-eye flight.

Has anyone in the history of the world ever taken an overnight flight Sunday evening when they had to be someplace Monday morning (be it a destination, or back home), and not felt like total garbage the whole day and maybe even into the next day too?

Seriously, ninety-nine times out of a hundred it is just not worth it. Yes, this is most often a cost-saving measure, and generally a quite effective one. But there are other ways to save money and save yourself the pain.

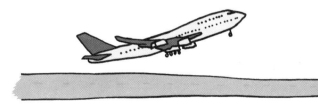

In fact, come back with a day or two to spare.

The luxury of having a day or two at home to do your laundry, get some groceries, and most of all just chill out upon returning from a trip can hardly be overstated.

Yes, of course we all want to stay gone as long as possible and pack as much vacationing in as we possibly can while we're there. But it turns out the best way to preserve that relaxed vacation feeling is not to zoom straight from the airport to work. Go figure.

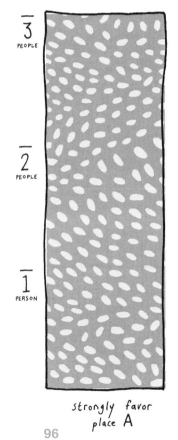

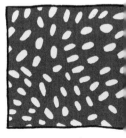

3 PEOPLE

2 PEOPLE

1 PERSON

strongly favor
place A

have agreed
to place A

genuinely have
no opinion

More walking, less talking.

When a group of five or more people is standing on the street corner trying to decide where to go for dinner (or breakfast, or drinks, or dancing, etc.*), anything better than a 75% consensus about where to go is plenty.

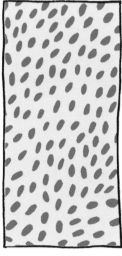

pretending to
have no opinion

strongly favor
place B

*This principle applies to a great many other things as well, besides going places, particularly the fine art of making group decisions at work.

Your body is talking to you.

LISTEN.

YOUR LYMPHATIC SYSTEM HELPS KEEP YOU FROM GETTING SICK.

Swollen glands in your neck can mean you're fighting something off. When this happens, it's a message telling you to take extra good care of yourself—get more sleep, eat healthy, drink fluids.

One of the key moments of being a grown-up is when someone you know has a baby.

Think about it: This is the first baby you are meeting as an adult (as opposed to younger cousins and whatnot you knew when you yourself were still a kid). That's a big deal.

When this momentous day arrives:

Don't be afraid to hold the baby.

Part of being a grown-up is being big. Big and competent and comforting. Being able to hold tiny new human beings against your chest is one of the greatest chances you're ever going to have to prove that.

The baby will most likely cry while you are holding it. This is not a big deal. Don't take it personally. The baby currently has one word in her vocabulary for expressing every single thing she needs to express and that word is "aaaaaugh!" Don't shove her back at her mom or dad the minute the crying starts, unless they clearly want you to. If the baby's caterwauling makes you anxious, just keep repeating to yourself:

I didn't make her I didn't break her

I didn't make her I didn't break her

I didn't make her I didn't break her

I didn't make her I didn't break her

I didn't make her I didn't break her

I didn't make her I didn't break her

I didn't make her I didn't break her

I didn't make her I didn't break her

I didn't make her I didn't break her

I didn't make her I didn't break her

I didn't make her I didn't break her

I didn't make her I didn't break her

ONLY COOK WITH WINE YOU'D ALSO LIKE TO DRINK.

Presumably you have some sort of personal mental guideline for the wine you enjoy imbibing. Maybe you'll quaff two buck plonk and maybe you won't. Maybe your preferred bottle is in the $5 or $10 or $15 range. Maybe you loathe Napa Valley Chardonnay and maybe you adore it. Likewise Merlot, Cabernet Sauvignon, rosé, and on and on. Whatever your preferences may be, they are totally fine.

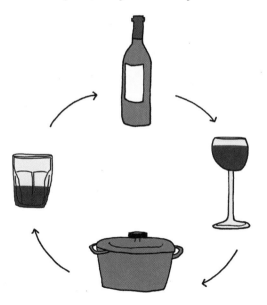

Other people's snobbery is not your problem.

LIKE WHAT YOU LIKE AND BE HAPPY.

Then, just apply your beverage parameters to any recipe you might be making that calls for wine as an ingredient, and your cooking will also be that much more to your own taste.

And don't forget to pour a little glass to enjoy while you're cooking.

Snappy dressers learn to distinguish between:

A) WHAT WILL ACTUALLY UP YOUR GAME, AND

B) WHAT'S JUST A BUNCH OF HYPE.

IF YOU'RE A GUY:

A) Learn your shirt size. Not just small, medium, or large, but the whole enchilada, with neck-circumference and arm-length measurements in inches. Being able to buy a shirt that actually fits is a very useful skill and will make you look sharp.

B) Going out and randomly getting your shoes shined will not make you feel like a million bucks. Shoe shines are great, but they only work if you get them done regularly.

IF YOU'RE A GIRL:

A) Get your boots reheeled. If you have a pair of boots you love that are wearing out, don't replace them—take them to the cobbler and get them polished and re-heeled and they'll be as good as new.

B) Don't bother getting measured for a bra. Everyone says to do this, but it's bogus. The way to find a good bra is to try on a whole bunch of bras. End of story.

Consider dryer sheets.

They may or may not turn out to be your thing, but they're totally worth a try. Here are a few things to reflect upon as you stand in the aisle of the grocery or drugstore, wondering whether to take the leap on buying a box. . . .

There are certain things that, if people grew up with them, they just automatically keep using, but if they did not grow up with them, then it just never occurs to them to try. Dryer sheets are one of these things.

There are certain little things that can bring surprisingly big happiness.

Dryer sheets are one of those things too.

Particularly if static cling is a big issue for you.

Or if you always wish your clothes were softer.

And bear in mind that "unscented" is totally an option.

A cheapo box of the little flimsy things has the potential to up your whole laundry game. You might go from feeling like a slob in a dorm to a full-fledged grown-up.

Potentially life changing.

Some of the best things you ever discover about yourself will be super counterintuitive.

FOR EXAMPLE:

People who are absolutely not morning people, like *at all*, make some of the best early risers. Huh? But for real: getting up in the morning is so horrifically awful for them—regardless of what time they do it—that they might as well get up earlier and have more time in their day, six a.m. being no worse than nine a.m. as far as they're concerned.

When you figure out such things about your own life and try to explain them to other people, they may look at you like you're crazy. No matter.

Just do what works for you and let the rest take care of itself.

As a wise woman once said:

If you're working all the time in the evenings and on the weekends—

THERE'S EITHER SOMETHING WRONG WITH YOUR JOB, OR SOMETHING WRONG WITH THE WAY YOU'RE DOING YOUR JOB.

Don't check work email at home.

They're not paying you enough to buy all your spare time and peace of mind.

Even if you think they are, they're not.

The freedom of your mind is beyond valuation.

This is why personal email accounts exist.

You don't need to have everything all at once.

ENJOY WHAT YOU'VE GOT...

EXAMPLES:

- A chocolate chip cookie
- A free day at the museum
- Beers with friends
- Dating
- A sunny Sunday afternoon in the park
- Fast fashion
- Trying new recipes
- Road trips
- Throwing parties
- The beach, lake, or river
- Sale shopping

... AND KEEP SOME STUFF TO LOOK FORWARD TO LATER.

- Tropical vacations
- The latest release phone or computer
- Stockings with seams up the back
- Living alone
- Fine dining
- High-quality wardrobe staples
- Your favorite authors' brand-new books in hardcover
- World travel
- All the snacks you want at the movies
- Marriage
- Built-in shelving

The vast majority of people will never again weigh what they did in high school.

NOR SHOULD THEY.

You wouldn't want to weigh what you did when you were six years old, would you? Ditto sixteen. You were not yet fully formed.

~~Wear swimming goggles while chopping onions~~

~~Hold a burnt match in your teeth while chopping onions~~

~~Refrigerate onions prior to chopping onions~~

~~Run onions under cold water while chopping onions~~

~~Eat bread while chopping onions~~

~~Rub lemon juice on your knife while chopping onions~~

~~Put a fan on the counter while chopping onions~~

~~Hold your breath while chopping onions~~

~~Use a super-sharp knife while chopping onions*~~

*Actually, this last one is a very good idea, but not for reasons having anything to do with the whole crying thing. Keeping your knife sharp will just make your life in the kitchen much better in general.

Nothing in this world, ever, anywhere, will stop you from crying when chopping onions.

Some people cry a lot, some a little.

Give up trying to fix this problem and move on with your life.

Or, as a wise man once said:

> Learn to hate onions,
> or learn to love crying.

OKAY, THIS RIGHT HERE MIGHT ACTUALLY BE THE NUMBER ONE
LESSON OF GROWN-UP-HOOD*:

You can't change your parents.

Or anyone.

So don't try.

(With any luck, they'll return the favor.)

*Oh, unless it's the champagne thing, or the deserving to be loved thing, or the thing about how no one is looking at you, or maybe the thing about the plane tickets. But if it's not any of those things, it's for sure this.

How to do the perfect high five:

You know how sometimes you go to high five some-one and you totally miss? If you look at the elbow on the arm of their oncoming hand—as opposed to look-ing at the hand itself, or their face, or anyplace else—you will land a perfect high five every single time.

That's right, the elbow.

Give it a try.

You're welcome.

Rules Are Often More Flexible than They Appear to Be.

Missed a deadline? Flubbed a meeting? Provided wrong information? There is nearly always a way to fix it.

And, related:

Get a Lot More Comfortable with Being Wrong.

HERE ARE JUST A FEW OF THE EXCEPTIONS TO THE THINGS IN THIS BOOK (OTHERWISE KNOWN AS PLACES WHERE THIS BOOK IS WRONG, OR AT LEAST NOT 100% RIGHT 100% OF THE TIME):

PAGE 32: The meat won't stop sticking when it's done if it's ground. Or if it's fish.

PAGE 94: Throw this one out the window the moment a truly awesome travel opportunity presents itself that requires you to fly overnight, and that, to you, feels worth the pain of doing so.

PAGE 16: In order to pass up getting onto the crowded transit vehicle in front of you, you must have actual visual confirmation, from your own eyeballs, that the second, less crowded bus or train is actually coming. Do not trust electronic prediction systems of any kind for this.

PAGE 36: When doing that thing with the spray paint? You don't actually need to sand. You do need to prime though.

PAGE 59: Ranch dressing.

BE WHO YOU ARE NOW.

You don't actually want to be forever young.

The older you get the more yourself you get to be.

And that is utterly fantastic.

ACKNOWLEDGMENTS

Thank you to my utterly delightful editor, Wynn Rankin, for encouraging me to write the book I've been meaning to write for over a decade, and then for helping me make it about a billion times better than I ever thought possible. Thank you to the very, very fine folks at Chronicle, including (but not limited to!) Emily, Rachel, Lia, Tamar, Michelle, Natalie, Sandy, April, Sarah M., Caitlin, and Christina. Thank you to my friends and family—particularly Shweta, Casey, Vanessa, Kristen, and my lovely parents—for always encouraging my wacky creative endeavors and offering both moral and practical support. Thank you to the awesome folks at Cup of Joe coffee house and Jane bakery, where this book was mostly written. And greatest thanks of all to Mabel and Bill, who make my grown-up life ridiculously awesome each and every day.